www.booksbyboxer.com

Bee Three Publishing is an imprint of Books By Boxer
Published by
Books By Boxer, Leeds, LS13 4BS, UK
Books by Boxer (EU), Dublin, D02 P593, IRELAND
Boxer Gifts LLC, 955 Sawtooth Oak Cir, VA 22802, USA
© Books By Boxer 2024
All Rights Reserved
MADE IN CHINA
ISBN: 9781915410573

MIX
Paper
FSC™ C007683

This book is produced from responsibly sourced paper to ensure forest management

WHY DID THE SCARECROW WIN AN AWARD?

BECAUSE HE WAS OUTSTANDING IN HIS FIELD.

DID YOU HEAR
ABOUT THE
CLAUSTROPHOBIC
ASTRONAUT?

**HE JUST
NEEDED
A LITTLE
SPACE!**

WHAT DO YOU
CALL AN ILLEGALLY
PARKED FROG?

TOAD!

WHAT DO YOU CALL A SHEEP ON A TRAMPOLINE?

A WOOLY JUMPER.

WHAT DO FROGS ORDER AT RESTAURANTS?

FRENCH FLIES.

EVERY MORNING I ANNOUNCE THAT I'M GOING JOGGING BUT THEN I DON'T GO...

IT'S A RUNNING JOKE!

WHY DON'T SKELETONS FIGHT EACH OTHER?

THEY DON'T HAVE THE GUTS!

WHAT DID YODA SAY WHEN HE SAW HIMSELF IN 4K?

HDMI

WHAT DID THE GRAPE SAY WHEN IT GOT CRUSHED?

NOTHING, IT JUST LET OUT A LITTLE WHINE.

I DON'T TRUST
THE TREES...

THEY SEEM
KIND OF
SHADY!

TO THE GUY WHO
INVENTED ZERO...

THANKS FOR
NOTHING!

DID YOU HEAR ABOUT THE CHEESE FACTORY THAT EXPLODED?

THERE WAS NOTHING LEFT BUT

DE BRIE!

I JUST GOT THROWN OUT OF MY LOCAL PARK FOR ARRANGING THE SQUIRRELS BY HEIGHT...

THEY DIDN'T LIKE MY **CRITTER SIZING!**

WHAT'S E.T. SHORT FOR?

BECAUSE HE'S ONLY GOT LITTLE LEGS!

LAST NIGHT
MY WIFE AND I
WATCHED TWO
MOVIES BACK
TO BACK.

**LUCKILY I
WAS THE
ONE FACING
THE TV.**

I WANTED TO BUY A PAIR OF CAMOUFLAGE PANTS...

BUT I COULDN'T FIND ANY.

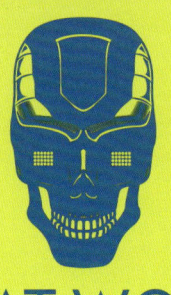

WHAT WOULD THE TERMINATOR BE CALLED IN HIS RETIREMENT?

THE EXTERMINATOR!

I GAVE AWAY
ALL MY USED
BATTERIES TODAY...

FREE OF CHARGE!

DOGS CAN'T
OPERATE MRI
MACHINES...

BUT CAT
SCAN!

WHY DO MELONS HAVE WEDDINGS?

BECAUSE THEY CANTALOUPE!

WHAT DID ONE HAT SAY TO THE OTHER?

WAIT HERE, I'M GOING ON AHEAD!

WHAT'S THE LOUDEST PET YOU CAN OWN?

A TRUMPET.

WHAT DID THE BUFFALO SAY TO HIS SON WHEN HE DROPPED HIM OFF AT SCHOOL?

BISON.

WHAT DID THE LEFT EYE SAY TO THE RIGHT?

SOMETHING SMELLS BETWEEN US.

WHY DO SWEDISH BATTLESHIPS HAVE BARCODES ON THEM?

SO THEY CAN SCANDINAVIAN.

I INVENTED A PENCIL WITH AN ERASER ON EACH END...

THERE'S NO POINT TO IT.

I ONCE WROTE A SONG ABOUT A TORTILLA...

BUT IT'S MORE OF A
WRAP.

I USED TO HATE FACIAL HAIR...

BUT IT GREW ON ME.

WHY WAS THE
LITTLE COOKIE SAD?

HIS MOTHER
WAS A WAFER
SO LONG.

WHY DID THE PICTURE GET ARRESTED?

IT GOT FRAMED.

WHAT DO YOU
CALL A COW WITH
NO LEGS?

GROUND
BEEF.

WHAT KIND OF COFFEE DOES A VAMPIRE DRINK?

DE-COFFIN-ATED.

A BOOK FELL ON MY HEAD...

I ONLY HAVE MY SHELF TO BLAME.

TWO GUYS
WALKED INTO
A BAR.

THE
THIRD GUY
DUCKED.

I LOST 25% OF
MY ROOF LAST
NIGHT...

OOF.

A MAGICIAN WAS WALKING DOWN THE STREET...

THEN HE TURNED INTO A **STORE.**

WHY ARE
ELEVATOR JOKES
SO GOOD?

THEY WORK ON MANY

LEVELS.

I HAD A DATE LAST NIGHT AND IT WAS PERFECT.

TOMORROW, I'LL HAVE A FIG.

SUNDAYS ARE
ALWAYS A LITTLE
SAD...

BUT THE DAY BEFORE
IS A
**SADDER
DAY.**

TWO WINDMILLS ARE STANDING ON A WIND FARM. ONE ASKS, 'WHAT'S YOUR FAVORITE KIND OF MUSIC?' THE OTHER REPLIES...

'I'M A BIG METAL FAN.'

HOW DO TREES GO ONLINE?

THEY JUST LOG ON!

WHEN IS A DOOR
NOT A DOOR?

WHEN IT'S AJAR.

WHAT'S AN ASTRONAUT'S FAVORITE BOARD GAME?

MOON -OPOLY.

WHY CAN'T YOU HEAR A PTERODACTYL GO TO THE BATHROOM?

THE P IS SILENT.

WHAT DO TOILETS DO WHEN THEY'RE EMBARRASSED?

THEY ALWAYS GET A BIT FLUSHED.

WHAT DO YOU CALL FAKE SPAGHETTI?

AN IMPASTA!

WHAT DO YOU CALL CHEESE THAT ISN'T YOURS?

NACHO CHEESE.

I'M READING A BOOK ON THE HISTORY OF GLUE...

I JUST CAN'T SEEM TO PUT IT DOWN!

WHAT DID ONE
PLATE SAY TO THE
OTHER PLATE?

DINNER'S
ON ME.

WHAT DID THE JANITOR SAY WHEN HE JUMPED OUT OF THE CLOSET?

SUPPLIES!

WHY DON'T
SEAGULLS FLY
OVER THE BAY?

BECAUSE THEN
THEY'D BE CALLED

BAGELS!

WHY DID THE TOMATO TURN RED?

BECAUSE IT SAW THE SALAD DRESSING!

DID YOU HEAR ABOUT THE ITALIAN CHEF WHO DIED?

HE PASTA WAY!

WHAT'S THE BEST THING ABOUT SWITZERLAND?

I DON'T KNOW, BUT THEIR FLAG IS A

BIG PLUS!

WHY SHOULD
YOU NEVER TRUST
A CARP'S EXCUSE?

THEY ALWAYS SEEM A
LITTLE
FISHY.

WHY IS IT SO CHEAP TO THROW A PARTY AT A HAUNTED HOUSE?

BECAUSE THE GHOSTS BRING THE BOOS.

DID YOU KNOW YOUR PUPILS ARE THE LAST PART TO STOP WORKING WHEN YOU DIE?

THEY DILATE.

HOW DO COWS
STAY UP TO DATE?

THEY READ THE

MOO-
SPAPER.

WHAT'S THE DIFFERENCE BETWEEN A WELL-DRESSED MAN ON A UNICYCLE AND A POORLY-DRESSED MAN ON A BICYCLE?

ATTIRE.

I HATE MY JOB—
ALL I DO IS CRUSH
CANS ALL DAY.

IT'S SODA
PRESSING.

I FOUND A
WOODEN SHOE IN
MY TOILET TODAY.

IT WAS
CLOGGED.

A MAN SAID TO HIS DOCTOR, "HELP ME, I THINK I'M SHRINKING!"

"NOW SETTLE DOWN," SAID THE DOCTOR...

"YOU'LL JUST HAVE TO LEARN TO BE A LITTLE PATIENT."

LANCE ISN'T THAT COMMON A NAME THESE DAYS, BUT IN MEDIEVAL TIMES...

THEY WERE CALLED LANCE-A-LOT.

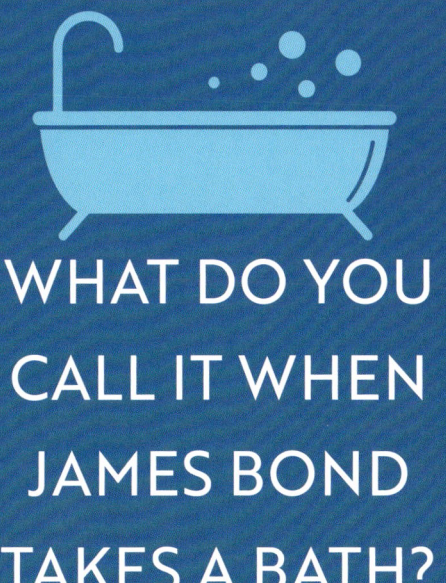

WHAT DO YOU CALL IT WHEN JAMES BOND TAKES A BATH?

BUBBLE 07.

WHAT DO YOU CALL SOMETHING THAT'S MADE FROM LEATHER AND SOUNDS LIKE A SNEEZE?

A SHOE!

I'M WRITING A
BOOK ON
REVERSE
PSYCHOLOGY...

PLEASE
DON'T
READ IT!

I USED TO BE
A BAKER...

BUT I DIDN'T
MAKE ENOUGH
DOUGH.

WHY DID THE
COFFEE FILE A
POLICE REPORT?

IT GOT
MUGGED.

WHY DON'T
SCIENTISTS TRUST
STAIRS?

BECAUSE THEY'RE ALWAYS
UP TO
SOMETHING.

WHAT DID THE BIG FLOWER SAY TO THE LITTLE FLOWER?

WHAT'S UP, BUD?

I'M FRIENDS WITH
25 LETTERS OF
THE ALPHABET.

I DON'T
KNOW
Y.

I USED TO PLAY
PIANO BY EAR...

BUT NOW
I USE MY
HANDS.

I TRIED TO MAKE UP A JOKE ABOUT GHOST BUT I COULDN'T...

IT HAD PLENTY OF

SPIRIT BUT NO BODY.

WHAT IS THE DIFFERENCE BETWEEN A PIANO AND TUNA?

YOU CAN
TUNA PIANO
BUT YOU CAN'T PIANO A TUNA.

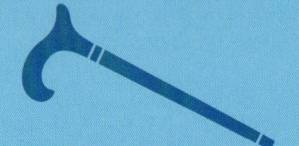

TODAY AT THE BANK, AN OLD LADY ASKED ME TO CHECK HER BALANCE...

SO I PUSHED HER OVER.

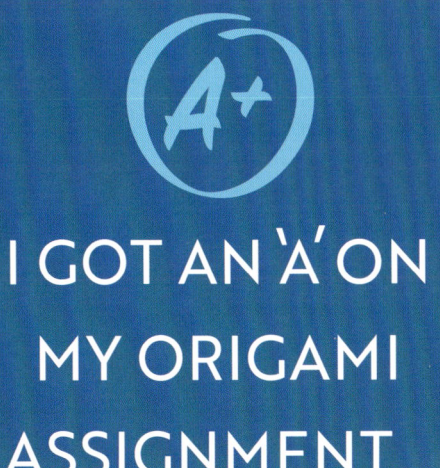

I GOT AN 'A' ON MY ORIGAMI ASSIGNMENT...

WHEN I TURNED MY PAPER INTO MY

TEACHER.

HOW MANY STORM TROOPERS DOES IT TAKE TO CHANGE A LIGHTBULB?

NONE, THEY'RE ALL ON THE

DARK SIDE.

HOW MUCH DOES A CHIMNEY COST?

NOTHING, IT'S ON THE HOUSE!

WHY DID THE
COFFEE TASTE
LIKE DIRT?

BECAUSE IT WAS

GROUND

JUST A FEW MINUTES
AGO.

WHAT DO YOU CALL A CRIMINAL LANDING AN AIRPLANE?

CONDESCENDING.

JUSTICE IS A DISH
BEST SERVED
COLD...

—————————————

OTHERWISE, IT'S JUST
WATER.

WHY SHOULD YOU NEVER THROW GRANDPA'S FALSE TEETH AT YOUR VEHICLE?

YOU MIGHT DENTURE CAR.

WHY ARE FIR TREES BAD AT KNITTING?

THEY ALWAYS DROP THEIR
NEEDLES.

WHY COULDN'T THE TREE GET ON HIS COMPUTER?

BECAUSE HE COULDN'T **LOG ON.**

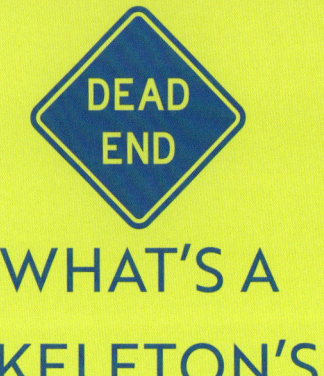

WHAT'S A SKELETON'S FAVORITE TYPE OF ROAD?

A DEAD END.

WHAT DID THE ALIEN SAY TO THE LANDSCAPER?

"TAKE ME TO YOUR WEEDER!"

WHAT DID THE MOTHER BROOM SAY TO THE BABY BROOM?

"IT'S TIME TO GO TO SWEEP."

THE OTHER DAY I WAS ATTACKED BY A BUNCH OF CIRCUS CLOWNS IN A PARKING LOT...

I WON THOUGH, CAUSE I WENT RIGHT FOR THE

JUGGLER.

HOW MANY EARS
DOES CAPTAIN
KIRK HAVE?

THREE.

THE LEFT EAR, THE
RIGHT EAR, AND THE
FINAL FRONT-EAR.

DID YOU HEAR
ABOUT THE
FAMOUS PICKLE?

HE'S A
REALLY BIG
DILL.

WHAT HAS FOUR WHEELS AND FLIES?

A GARBAGE TRUCK.

YOU DON'T NEED A PARACHUTE TO GO SKYDIVING...

YOU NEED ONE TO GO SKYDIVING TWICE.

HOW DO YOU
MAKE 7 EVEN?

TAKE
AWAY
THE S.

WHY IS SAUSAGE BAD FOR YOU?

IT BRINGS OUT THE WURST IN PEOPLE.

WHY DID THE TEDDY BEAR TURN DOWN A SLICE OF CAKE?

HE WAS STUFFED.